NAKED
PARENTING
7 KEYS TO RAISING KIDS WITH CONFIDENCE

LEAH DECESARE

Library of Congress Cataloging-in-Publication Data
is available.

Printed in the United States of America
Published by Mother's Circle, LLC

Cover design: Nick DeCesare
Interior design and composition: Nick DeCesare
Author photo: Matt Wronski

ISBN: 978-0-9905322-0-0

www.motherscircle.net

To my parents,
For their parenting example
and for their unending support

To my husband,
My very best friend

To our children,
Ali, Michael and Anna,
For their laughter and love

Acknowledgments

Thank you to past clients and friends who have encouraged me to write down my parenting philosophies.

Thank you to my early readers: Beth Bogdan, Kara Ratigan, Dana Marnane, and Becky Grills. This book is better because of their feedback.

To my high-tech, creative daughter, Ali, for her help in making the *Naked Parenting* book trailer.

Thank you to Robin Kall Homonoff for her friendship, support and wealth of great ideas.

Thank you to my husband for his ceaseless support and for sending me away for solitary writing weekends. And thank you to my parents for letting me use their house for those weekends, and for always believing in me.

Contents

Introduction

Naked Parenting is parenting stripped down to the bare basics focusing on seven keys to raising kids who are self-sufficient, confident, respectful, and resilient. Nudity not required. Confidence and genuine self love, without believing the world owes you anything, is the cornerstone of happy adulthood. And isn't that our main job as parents - to raise happy, fulfilled adults?

Naked Parenting approaches parenting in an honest, direct and realistic way. Guiding children with love, nurturing their strengths and self-image, and instilling personal responsibility are at the heart of Naked Parenting. There are thousands of topics that fall under the parenting umbrella, and so many I haven't jumped into here, but Naked Parenting addresses key concepts to help you raise confident, joyful, and well-adjusted kids, and to enjoy doing it.

We'll discuss love, honesty, communication, responsibility, discipline, mistakes and gratitude. You'll see how these ideas overlap, interrelate and reinforce one another. Learning these principles will help you to apply them across the myriad of parenting scenarios.

As a parent since 1998, a childbirth educator since 2002, and a doula since 2007, I have worked with hundreds of families as they transition to parenthood, or added another child to their family, and have witnessed a broad spectrum of parenting styles. As a mother of three children, one elementary-aged child and two teenagers, I have seen an even greater range of parenting techniques.

Every parent has their own style and the principles of Naked Parenting can fit into, and work in conjunction with, many ways of parenting. Use the ideas here with your own family rules, values and culture.

I have read countless parenting books and blogs, and I have written about parenting at www.MothersCircle.net since 2012. My clients continue to reach out to me for advice as their babies become toddlers and kindergarteners. Questions and comments from mothers through my blog have offered me the opportunity to share snip-its of my parenting philosophy, but Naked Parenting is the product of many suggestions and requests to "write a book," from clients and blog readers.

You will have your opinions about the ideas here. Good. We're all individuals and see the world from our own experiences. You may disagree with me. It's okay, don't follow that bit of advice. In parenthood, as in so much else in life, we need a box full of tools to choose from, tools for different situations, different kids, different ages, and even different days of the week. Sometimes a technique that works Monday doesn't work Wednesday, but try it again next week or next month, and you may find success with it.

The overall principles of Naked Parenting boil down to openness and honesty rooted in love. Not much to debate there, and I believe all parents can benefit from the ideas in this book.

Sometimes it feels like I'm going against the grain of current parenting fashions and norms. I'm much less strict than my parents or grandparents, but I often feel much stricter than many of my peers. And frankly, I don't like the word "strict," we have expectations for our children's behavior and we hold our kids accountable.

My husband and I have been criticized by other parents for doling out deserved consequences to our children, and some family members have balked at our Naked Parenting style even while bragging about how well-behaved and respectful our kids are. Another parent once said to me, "Aw, really, I can't believe you're not letting her go to the party, everyone's going." But my daughter lost that privilege, fair and square. She earned the consequence and, no, she didn't go to the party even though it stunk for me, for her, and for her friends.

Because of our follow through, our kids have learned that we mean what we say. They have adapted their behaviors, have apologized, and have grown from these hard-to-deliver responses to their actions.

That's right, Naked Parenting isn't easy, but as grown-ups, we need to take it on. It's up to us to deal with our own emotions and fears to be able to best parent our kids. Starting young with Naked Parenting will return valuable results. While the challenges shift and change as children get older, the basic groundwork will benefit you so that you can build on earlier lessons as children mature. If you're picking this up and your kids are already older, you can still add these elements to your parenting tool box.

Be prepared to commit, to make mistakes and to feel some resistance. You'll see the returns in greater family harmony, and in happier, more confident children.

Mistakes are part of this gig. Parenting is one big experiment, but as you'll see in Naked Mistakes, what matters is how we handle them. We all mess up. There is so much that is unpredictable in parenting that it's impossible to know what to do in every situation, but using the principles of Naked Parenting will help guide you as you apply them to the infinite number of scenarios you face as parents.

Naked Parenting takes energy; boundless, creative, energy. Many of the suggestions in this book will take time, will ask you to pause and reflect, will take some patience or some additional steps, but it's worth it. Your kids are worth it, your family is worth it and you are worth it. You will be rewarded many times over by doing the work.

So, let's get naked!

Chapter 1

What is Naked Parenting?

Parents set the tone for the family; harmonious or critical, joyful or angry, supportive or disinterested, open or shutoff. It's up to us, as parents, to foster and build the culture we want in our homes.

Who's in charge in your family? If you're the solid authority, you're one step ahead. This book will reinforce and invigorate your parenting and provide you with concrete tips and advice for raising confident, self-sufficient, and resilient kids.

If you have any inkling that it's not you in charge and that your kids hold most of the power, this book will help you reclaim (or claim in the first place) your rightful position in your family as leader, guide, and as the parents.

I am all about guilt-free parenting. We are doing our best and we want to be good moms and dads. The fact that you're reading this demonstrates your desire to be the best parent you can be, so give yourself a break. Even if, as you read, you realize that you have given up too much control to the little ones in your home, know that you can change things for the better, starting now. You can become a Naked Parent, too, and confidently guide your children into a successful, fulfilling adulthood.

Parenting is a learned skill. It's an ongoing education as kids enter new ages and stages. You're wise to be seeking out other ideas, tips, and thoughts on how to approach this lifelong, infinitely important job. I always tell my clients to read, research, learn, and then evaluate the information to determine how it can work in their family. Take what works, leave behind what doesn't.

There are many ways to parent and many effective styles. Families have different rules and values on bedtimes, homework, curfews, television, meals and so on. The Naked Parenting principles can be applied within the multitude of unique ways to parent.

Resources for parents abound and I continue to glean new strategies to try in our home. Reading parenting books and blogs can be useful in searching for answers to a specific parenting challenge. They can serve as motivation to kick it up, as encouragement, or as a reminder of things we already know we should be doing but have let slip.

Getting Naked

First, let's address what you might be thinking of as the literal aspect of Naked Parenting. You may be the kind of family that mills about unclothed or who all get dressed behind locked doors, or you may fall somewhere in between. In our family, anyone going through puberty has taken the lock-and-key approach and has stopped allowing anyone near a fitting room or bathroom. Coming out on the other side of adolescence has seen a loosening of these restrictions and some decreased modesty.

Every family will have their own comfort levels with nudity. If you're comfortable showering with toddlers or walking around in your undies with teens, the best way to know if it's okay for your family is to ask them. Wide open, up front, and direct communication, especially when it could be uncomfortable, is a basic tenant of Naked Parenting. Ask. Then model respect for the thoughts and feelings of others.

So, whether you throw on a robe, or drip down the hall in your birthday suit, let's move on to the figurative aspects of Naked Parenting. Get ready to get bare!

Parenting Goals

Why do we have kids? Simply, we decide to have children

for the prospect of a relationship. We have kids to love, to hold tight, to share our passions, our lives, and to teach and guide another human being. The ultimate goal of parenting is to raise children into adults who are happy, resilient, responsible, confident, and successful in whatever way we, or they, define that, and to enjoy it along the way. That can sound like a challenging task - and it is. I believe it is the greatest responsibility, and the greatest joy, in life.

On our way to raising responsible, fulfilled adults, we should delight in the journey. Naked Parenting allows you to appreciate, and find gratification in, those relationships. We should want to spend time with the children we're raising. Of course, there will be the tough and crummy times as parents, the challenging and stinky times. But overall, if you put in the work, you will reap the rewards in the form of courteous, well-behaved kids who are a pleasure to be around.

When I went away to college, I remember the shocking realization that not everyone had the same confidence I did. Living with others from around the country, I saw insecurities, anxieties, worries and self-deprecation in a way I had not noticed in high school. Even confident people can feel worried or off-balance, but there's a difference in that a truly confident person will not be crippled by fears or nerves but will step out in spite of them. It was at the beginning of college when I saw what my parents had taught me. I always felt loved, and that is the foundation of confidence, but I realized then, that the greatest gift they gave me was in nurturing and building self-confidence.

What does it take to raise confident kids? We need to love them openly, generously, and prolifically. We need to speak with them honestly and with clear expectations. We need to offer specific, concrete, and earned praise, not empty compliments. We need to discipline them from early on; positive discipline is necessary and critical in teaching children and in building their confidence. We need to model and teach them personal responsibility, manners, and gratitude, and we need to apologize when we really screw up.

Naked Parenting will support you as you work toward raising resilient, productive adults, even if they're only two years old right now. We only have our kids in our homes for eighteen short years, and as we near the day when our oldest daughter will leave for college, I can tell you, the old adage is true: With children, the days are long but the years are short. Raising amazing adults starts when we first hold those babies in our arms.

You Set the Example

To be a Naked Parent, you first need to get honest with yourself. Are you ready to step up, to be the parent, and to set a positive example? Often, the right thing to do is the harder thing to do. Telling your boss she's got lettuce in her teeth, turning in the diamond bracelet you found, returning the extra $20 the cashier accidentally gave you, sitting with a friend who just lost her baby. All tough, and all the right choice.

We need to examine, evaluate, and really assess ourselves to be the example for our children. We don't do this once and we're done, but we have to keep on doing it. I often find that my tone of voice can come out so snippy with our oldest child. So why am I shocked when I hear that tone right back at me? I need to acknowledge that it stems from me. I've modeled that for her and to help make a positive change, it needs to start with me. That's when I write notes to myself, work to be mindful of my speech and ask my husband to give me a signal when I'm talking with an edge to my voice. Bringing it to my consciousness allows me to change my behaviors and set a better example and a happier tone for my relationship with her.

In the same way, a healthy self-image as a parent helps us to project that to our children. It's important to model respect for one's own body, for your spouse or partner, and for your children and their bodies. Do you model healthy eating, staying fit, and good nutrition or do you eat cheese puffs as you try to persuade your kids to eat broccoli? Do you find yourself being critical of your own body, talking about yourself as fat or unattractive? Do you joke about needing a drink to cope, do you laugh about how you're dying for that glass of wine? Kids hear that and it shapes their own sense of self. You can enjoy your wine or your junk food, but be nakedly honest with yourself, and with your kids. Talk about things and be aware of what your words and actions convey.

Often among adults, in a casual, easy way, drinking is held high as a standard for a fun source of entertainment, it can be thrown around in innocence and light jesting. To children, that gives a very strong message, one we probably don't want or intend to relay. Being aware of this, my husband and I have made it a habit, especially as the kids have grown older, to not talk as if alcohol is important to having fun. Be mindful of what you're modeling and how your actions and words may influence your children's choices, impressions, and behaviors at all ages.

As with everything in parenting, repetition is necessary. Every message will need to be repeated over the years, over and over, in various forms, styles and from different directions. Not much is ever a one-time conversation or lesson. Our example, how we conduct ourselves, is one way of sharing and repeating our values and lessons.

Years before any discussions on drugs, eating disorders, alcohol or the birds and the bees, children must learn to respect and care for their bodies. An innate love of themselves and their physical form is the foundation for later decisions.

Self-respect is vital to model for our children. Self-worth starts young and ultimately guides tween and teen choices on smoking, drinking, sex, and many other things they'll face. Interactions in dating and among peers will be influenced by how much a teen values herself and her body. That self-image and respect is taught and nurtured at home.

You are the single greatest influence in your children's lives, even in the know-it-all teen years. You are parenting and teaching with your every action. From the first early moments of parenting, you're making decisions that affect your children and their choices and behaviors. Recognizing this will allow you to evaluate and alter your own behavior and attitude to project what you value and want your kiddos to learn.

What is Naked Parenting? Top Tips:

- Parents set the tone in their family.

- Nudity within a family is a personal decision. Openly discuss everyone's comfort level.

- The goal of parenting is to raise adults who are happy, resilient, responsible, confident and successful.

- Parenting should be enjoyable.

- If you put in the work, you will reap the rewards.

- We need to examine, evaluate and assess ourselves.

- Parents set the example for their children and model self-respect and family values.

- In parenting, repetition is necessary. Every message will need to be repeated.

- You are the single greatest influence on your children's lives, even in the teen years.

- Know that you are parenting and teaching with your every action.

It's not only children who grow. Parents do too. As much as we watch to see what our children do with their lives, they are watching us to see what we do with ours. I can't tell my children to reach for the sun. All I can do is reach for it, myself.

- Joyce Maynard

The hardest part of raising a child is teaching them to ride bicycles. A shaky child on a bicycle for the first time needs both support and freedom. The realization that this is what the child will always need can hit hard.

- Sloan Wilson

Chapter 2

Naked Love

Loving our kids is the basis for Naked Parenting. You love your kids. That's easy. It's simple, so why is there a whole chapter on love? There are times it can feel challenging. We know we love them, but in that instant, we may not be swelling with affection. You know the moments: when the baby won't stop crying or won't fall asleep (ever!), when your toddler pushes a child at the playground or wets his pants for the 78th time that day, when your eight year old bickers endlessly with her brother or your teen spits words at you like you were her greatest enemy. We may not feel very loving at those times, and really, that's okay. It's another forgive-yourself-moment.

We've all been there. It's okay to love your child but not to like them so much in a particular situation, but what's most important is that our children understand that no matter what, we love them.

From the time they were little, we've repeated this mantra to our kids, especially when they've acted out or had a doozy of a tantrum: "Nothing you can do or say will make me stop loving you." Never, ever, ever! Kids must know, without question, that no matter how angry you get, no matter how frustrated, no matter how naughty or cranky they've been, that no matter what happens, you love them and will always love them.

That's unconditional love in action.

Disciplining kids, guiding their behavior, and teaching them, is critical. It's another way of demonstrating your love for them, but before a boundary is ever set, children must know they are loved, without a doubt.

Douse them in kisses. Let the "I love you's" flow. Smoosh them in hugs and be present. Nakedly express your love. Love them grandly, fully, joyfully. For some people, outward displays of love may be hard. Remember, the right thing is often the hard thing. Even if you didn't grow up with gushing demonstrations of love, you can start with your children. It's okay to start in small steps, but whatever you do, be sure they know without hesitation or doubt that you love them, and physical proof of that does matter. A loving touch is a powerful thing.

Giving kids our undivided attention, and being genuinely

present, shows them they are valuable. Actively, attentively listening to them, from their worries and fears to their silly stories, and their long, long, long retelling of dreams, lets them know they matter to you. If you're unable to fully pay attention to them when they seek you out, explain that, and then make sure to get back to them at the very first opportunity you have to be 100% focused on them.

When kids are little, the amount of time we spend with them can feel overwhelming. How much they need from us just to get through the morning can be draining. The care-taking aspects of parenting in the early years are exhausting. Within that intensity of time, though, you'll find the joy when you slow down and take time each day to just *be* with your child. Look carefully at the dandelion he's showing you, really look into her eyes and hear what she's saying. Grasp those moments. They nurture you both.

As kids get older, deliberately make the time to sit and talk, and to call them over for a hug and a chat. Teens still need hugs and physical affection from their parents. Even if they seem to shun it, keep working on it. Give them a rub on the back, a squeeze of the hand, a kiss on the cheek because touch connects us.

Make time to be together, focused on one another. Turn off your cell phones or leave them in the other room so neither of you can get distracted by a ting or twang, then look into your child's eyes and talk. Take an interest in their interests, in their friends, in their lives. Your kids will know they are cherished and loved.

When I was a young mom, my dad told me, "Don't hold back hugs until they do something you want. Don't ever withhold your love." I've lived by that and, even now, after a heated scenario with a teenager, I will often calmly ask, even when I don't feel like it, "Do you need a hug?" Sometimes they grumble and cannot accept it at that moment, but inevitably, they return ready to claim their hug. It helps heal and reconnect us after an argument or the unwelcome delivery of a consequence.

Other ways to make kids feel special and loved are to send notes in their lunches, schedule one-on-one time with each child and with each parent, and to notice the good things they do. Keep a list of all the wonderful things you witness, large and small, and write them into a note to share at the end of the week. Get on their level if they're little, or have them sit if they're taller, and make eye contact. It's powerful to look your child in the eye and tell them why you love them.

A child who knows she is loved can step out into the world with confidence. Knowing they are loved allows kids the freedom to explore, to take risks, to venture out and learn, grow and change the world.

Naked Love Top Tips:

- Tell your kids: "Nothing you can do or say will make me stop loving you."

- Shower kids with physical love. Pour on the kisses, hugs and "I love yous."

- Make time daily to give kids your undivided attention.

- Teens need hugs, focused attention, and active listening from their parents.

- Don't withhold love.

- Spend one-on-one time with each child.

Kids spell love T-I-M-E.

- John Crudele

There really are places in the heart you don't even know exist until you love a child.

- Anne Lamott,

Operating Instructions: A Journal of My Son's First Year

Chapter 3

Naked Honesty

Another foundation of Naked Parenting is honesty. Being truthful in interactions with your kids is modeling your expectations and values for them, and it builds a solid base for everything else you do.

Naked Honesty in Praise

Be honest in your praise and assessment of your children's strengths and weaknesses. For example, at the middle school talent show last year, more than one child got up on that stage and, with great enthusiasm, sang horribly. Even if they didn't know it, the audience embarrassment for the kids was palpable. I feel it was the parents' responsibility to have been honest with their child. Telling them they can sing when they can't doesn't build self-esteem or help them in anyway, instead, it's doing them a disservice.

If a child loves singing but it's not their greatest asset, I might encourage lessons or opportunities to improve or to simply enjoy singing, but I would also gently and kindly let them know that this isn't one of the things they're awesome at. There are always things our kids *are* awesome at, and helping them to identify and discover them is part of our job.

Hard work and determination are critical life skills and top on our list of family values. If a child is really in love with an activity, they will put in the hours and slog through the not-fun parts to get better. It's important for kids to have a broad array of experiences and to have many different areas where they feel competent and successful. Providing kids with varied opportunities is enriching. Allowing them to guide the activities, to select and have control over which they participate in, will promote their sense of self.

In our family, we highly value down time; time for kids to just play, create, run and imagine. I believe in avoiding over-scheduling and under-playing. It's all about balance. With activities, our rule has always been that we ask and offer different options to the kids and they can decide. "Do you want to play soccer, lacrosse, tennis? Do you want to take painting, sewing, horseback riding, piano?" Clearly, this is all within reason and with consideration for the family's finances and the scheduling of activities for multiple children.

Building in free time, family time and unstructured time is just as important as providing opportunities for kids to gain new experiences and build their skills in sports, music and other enrichment activities.

Continue to offer things, new and old, as opportunities present themselves, and allow the kids to decide if they'd like to participate or not. Our rule is that once a child says yes, she has committed to that activity or team for the length of the term. There is no complaining about going to games or practices and there is no quitting, but if they didn't like it, the next time around, they can choose to not sign up again.

Offer praise for trying something new and for sticking to it even though they may not have liked it. It's important to give detailed praise about how they improved, how you noticed a kind act they did for a team mate or how hard they worked to memorize all the lines for the school play.

Praise should be earned. When you compliment your child, be specific; let them know you were really paying attention. Giving them honest, precise praise allows them to see themselves in a positive light and to build upon that. Being recognized for including another child or for taking a breath and calming down before speaking will encourage them to continue to do those behaviors. It's a positive cycle. Noticing the good will increase the good.

Baseless praise feels hollow to children, they figure it out and eventually it serves to make them feel less confident. They might even feel bad about themselves, sensing the insincerity from a parent and feeling fraudulent.

Instead of saying, "You're a great artist," or "You played great," it's much more valuable to comment on how long they concentrated on the project, how they passed the ball well, or how the way they thanked the coach showed good manners and appreciation.

I have no problem telling my kids that a piece of art, or school work, or the way they played a game wasn't their best. I tell them with kindness, and most of the time, they nod or smile with recognition that they already knew it wasn't. Saying, "It's not my favorite drawing you've done," is not going to shatter a child, instead, she'll know that when I say, "I love this painting and the colors you chose for the butterfly, I can tell you worked hard on this," that I mean it.

A child knows when she didn't try her best or do well, and being honest doesn't mean kicking a kid when they're down, it doesn't even mean being critical. It simply means not lying to your kids about their abilities or fluffing them up without substance.

Naked Honesty in Emotions

Being honest in our emotions is important for both kids

and adults. I loved the years when the kids were young and we taught them the names for different feelings, encouraging them to show their happy face, their angry face, their sad face, and my favorite with each kid, their surprised face. I can still see those wide-eyes and the funny-circled mouths.

Labeling emotions helps children feel more secure, allows them to better communicate what's going on inside and it also helps us, as parents, to manage our own feelings. If we're feeling rushed, stressed or worried, it's helpful to acknowledge and address those feelings before interacting with our kids. Of course, it's not always possible or realistic to be able to be alone until we're ready to communicate calmly, but mindfulness of our own emotional state helps us to adjust our responses, it minimizes overreacting and short tempers.

Even at young ages, kids understand when we're honest about our feelings. Explain that, "Mommy's feeling sad, that's why I'm crying," or "Mommy's feeling very angry, I need to be alone for a minute to calm down." This teaches children that their parents, too, have feelings and needs, and reinforces the lessons about sharing and controlling their own emotions. It's another opportunity to model the way for our children and is much more educational, and less scary, than saying, "I'm fine," or "Nothing's wrong," when they can tell otherwise. Practice emotional honesty.

It's important to allow kids to feel unpleasant emotions

like frustration, disappointment, rejection, or exclusion. We can hug them, hold their hand, cry with them through it but we cannot rescue them or take it away. Supporting them and validating their feelings is more important than trying to fix it or take away the intense emotions.

Life's Not All About the Kids

As kids get older, it's okay for them to know they are not the center of the universe. Can you tell I have two teenagers? Inherently, all children, toddlers to teens, are self-centered, it's part of biology and growing up, but it's okay for them to know their parents are people, too, with feelings and needs. Allow your needs to come first, too. Take time to prioritize and nurture yourself and your relationship with your spouse or partner.

For more, see the bonus material at the end of the book including *Why You Need Mommy Time* and *Nurturing the Couple*.

It's not just okay, it's a positive lesson, for them to sometimes wait for you to pick them up because you're working on a big project or driving another child somewhere. It's okay, and even good, for them to hear about all the things you do in a day to keep your family running.

The recognition that mom grocery shopped, read food labels, put it all in the cart, then out of the cart to pay, then back in the cart, then out of the cart into the car, then out of the car into the house, then into the pantry and fridge all before even cooking dinner can help older kids appreciate the back-end work that goes into their meals. I don't harp on it or tell the kids constantly everything I do for them (we'd never have enough hours, plus someday, they'll learn for themselves, firsthand) but a mention every so often, not to induce guilt or to seek praise but to create awareness, is helpful to give kids perspective. Recognizing and appreciating others are important lessons in empathy.

Do you bend over backwards to accommodate your children's wishes? I see many parents catering to their kid's every whim or tiptoeing around in fear of upsetting their child, worried about an impending tantrum. In adopting the Naked Parenting philosophy, you'll build your own parenting confidence and you'll feel secure and better equipped to handle whatever your kids throw your way. Apply this at mealtime, playtime, bedtime and all day long. For example, make one meal for dinner for everyone and anyone who doesn't care for it doesn't have to eat it but they don't get another meal instead. Kids learn fast. It's good for them not to get everything they want when they want it.

If you're bored silly watching the kids dunk underwater

for the 63rd time then it's okay to call them over to you, tell them that you've enjoyed seeing their new trick and you're happy they're having fun, but now you, too, would like to have fun, so you're going to sit and read your book or talk with your friends. Don't lose who you are in the mix of parenting. Be true to yourself as a parent, that's Naked Honesty and it makes you stronger.

Naked Honesty in Actions

Be honest in your actions. Align your actions with your values and follow through on what you say.

Do you teach your kids to be kind to others but then yell at the driver in front of you? Do you teach your kids to wait until their mouths are empty to talk but then talk with your mouth full? Do you teach your kids to be honest but then lie about their age at the museum to get them in for free?

Naked Honesty in your actions demonstrates integrity and is another form of that needed repetition to help kids learn and integrate those lessons. And for the love of God, if you say you're going to do something, DO IT!

Whether it's negative or positive, if you tell your kids you're going to do something, act honestly. I, personally, almost never use the word, "I promise," unless I know without question that I can keep that promise. I do promise that I will always love them, no matter what they do or say (see Naked Love). Never make a promise you can't keep. Even without using the word "promise," be honest in your actions.

If you give kids an allowance, pay them on time. If you tell your daughter you'll take her to the park or shopping for new soccer cleats that weekend, take her. Life throws things at us and sometimes it becomes too complicated or busy to do what you said you would in that timeframe, this is where Naked Communication comes in. Explain the situation, brainstorm solutions, find another time to do what you agreed to and then execute. Only one reschedule allowed. Take time for a self-assessment if you find yourself habitually breaking commitments to your kids. It's as trite as it is true: Actions speak louder than words.

Naked honesty in your actions applies to the flip side, too. If you say, "If you do that one more time, we're leaving the playground," then you need to leave if the kid does it one more time. Too many parents are frustrated that their kids don't listen the first time, but by giving their kids extra chances to listen, they've actually taught their kids not to listen the first time. If you leave when you say you're going to leave, guess what? The next time, that kid is going to remember and will hop to when you say hop to. They'll know mommy or daddy means it when she/he says it.

If you tell your child that he will lose the computer until he empties the dishwasher, follow through and be sure he doesn't get access to the computer (or DS, or phone apps, or Game Cube) until he's done the job you asked him to do. Kids learn from swift, prompt, and consistent action. Naked Honesty in your actions will help kids correlate cause and effect, understanding that, "When I do X, then Y happens."

Talking, by the way, is not action. Talking at a child, going on about what they did wrong and how you feel about it, is not going to be as effective as acting. There is a time for debriefing and discussion, but if a child crosses a limit you set, you must act decisively and leave the talk for another time. That is Naked Honesty in action.

A Note About Bunnies, Fairies, and Men in Red Suits

In our family, we have always been visited by Santa Claus, the Easter Bunny and the Tooth Fairy. Much of parenting is a judgement call and should reflect each family's values and beliefs. To us, this tradition doesn't breech honesty, to other families, it may.

When our oldest daughter learned we were behind the workings of these characters, in two phases, she cried and was disappointed, even though she'd had an underlying inkling. Then she wiped her tears and said, with maturity surpassing her age, "Now I can focus on what Easter is really about!" Wow! Okay, that went well.

A little later, she connected the dots and understood about Santa, too. That episode was a bit bumpier and gave me pause to evaluate. I wondered if we had broken her trust. She yelled, "You lied to me!" Ouch! Had we lied to her?

Whenever the kids have asked around the periphery of the Big Question, I always simply responded, "What do you think?" or sometimes, "Yes, I believe in Santa," and I do as I witness the generosity and outpouring for those in need.

Once our daughter was in on the magic, though, helping me out, she got it. She no longer felt lied to but instead felt grateful for the tradition. So, for us, we continue.

More Naked Honesty

Being honest and sincere in your interactions with your children shows your respect for them and earns their respect for you. Kids know when people aren't being honest with them.

Set the standard for honesty in your home. From early on, teach kids that your expectation is honesty, even if it's hard to tell the truth about something. Fostering a climate of truthfulness in your family begins with parents modeling honesty.

The value of honesty crosses all areas of life from school, grades, friends, and first jobs, and that expectation is the bedrock of all relationships.

When kids feel secure with their emotions they can learn to feel them, manage them, express them, and work through the tough ones. Many adults aren't proficient at Naked Emotions, so the ability to identify and claim their feelings is a gift to give your children starting at a young age. Labeling and then experiencing emotions is healthy and allows healing and growth through difficult and overwhelming times.

Kids who can read others' emotions and who can understand that people around them have feelings, too, learn empathy. Being able to place themselves in another's position is a powerful practice. Confidence in their emotional abilities, in the limits their parents set, and in knowing their parents' words and actions are honest, all build a solid groundwork for children to become resilient, well-adjusted adults.

Naked Honesty Top Tips:

- Be honest in your praise and assessment of your children's strengths and weaknesses.

- Praise should be earned. When you compliment your child, be specific.

- Noticing good will increase the good.

- Being honest doesn't mean being critical.

- Being honest in our emotions is important for both kids and adults.

- Avoid over-scheduling and under-playing.

- It's okay for kids to know they are not the center of the universe.

- Don't lose who you are in being a parent. Be true to yourself.

- Align your actions with your values and the lessons you teach your children.

- If you say you're going to do something, do it!

- Kids learn from swift, prompt, and consistent action.

- Talking is not action.

- The value of honesty crosses all areas of life and is the bedrock of all relationships.

- It's a gift to your kids to teach them to identify and work through their feelings.

It is one thing to show your child the way, and a harder thing to then stand out of it.

- Robert Brault

Good, honest, hardheaded character is a function of the home. If the proper seed is sown there and properly nourished for a few years, it will not be easy for that plant to be uprooted.

- George A. Dorsey

Chapter 4

Naked Communication

Building upon the foundation of unwavering love and mindful honesty, open communication is the next block of Naked Parenting.

Clear Expectations

It's important to be clear and transparent about your expectations of your kids. From the time they are little, kids should know their boundaries and expected behaviors. These will adjust as kids grow, and parents need to clearly communicate the expectations as they change.

The way you state your expectations also matters. When our oldest was about 18 months, I cheerfully directed her to stop touching a plant. My mother pointed it out to me saying that if I'm scolding her or want her to understand what she's doing is wrong, I needed to use a firm voice, not a sweet voice. That single change made a marked difference in how I parented and communicated from that point on.

There are many tools to help kids understand the rules and values of your home. Through the years we've used various checklists and sticker charts. When the kids were little, each item was illustrated with a picture, and the kids could look at their list to see what they needed to do before preschool in the morning or after they got home. Things like brushing teeth and putting shoes in the basket have been required in our home since an early age.

We often joke that we're not trying to trip anyone up, it's pretty much the same thing every day. We expect personal hygiene activities, hand washing, teeth brushing and showering (with soap and shampoo, something I never thought I'd need to give reminders on), but we also have basic expectations of conduct, such as being kind to others, helping out around the house, listening when they're called, and speaking respectfully.

The kids know the expectations, large and small, and while there's no magic formula to have them all adhered to all the time (remember that repetition thing), they can also expect to be interrupted from whatever they're doing to come and take care of whatever they neglected to do.

Kids need to be able to anticipate cause and effect. For

example, they should be able to predict, "If I leave my coat on the floor, Mom's going to make me stop playing and come hang it up," or, "If I yell at my sister, I won't be allowed to play with her anymore." We want kids, starting young, to learn that they control their actions and because of that, they have control over the outcome. As they get older, this gets more complex, but the lesson remains: you can always control your response and reactions to circumstances. You alone are in charge of your attitude. You are in charge of whether you look outside yourself or within yourself for both fault and credit.

Clearly stating, repeating, and providing ways for children to understand their parents' expectations is key in Naked Communication.

Open for Questions

We want our children to be able to come to us with questions, any questions, from why is the sky blue to where do people go when they die. Open communication throughout their lives fertilizes the ground for when kids are older and the stakes are higher. Children should know they can get honest answers from their parents about anything: a word they don't understand that they heard on the bus, ideas on what to say to a boy who they're interested in, or an explanation for something their friends were talking about Friday night. We're open for business, the message to kids should be: Ask me anything, I will answer you honestly. Questions give parents opportunities to share their values and beliefs.

It's important to take the time to really listen to our kids, to answer them thoughtfully, and look up any answers we don't know. That's an opportunity to show them resourcefulness and how to go about seeking answers. By accident, our family has initiated "YouTube Moments." Whenever there's a question we don't know, or when a reference comes up in discussion that the kids don't understand, we look it up.

Because of these YouTube Moments, they've learned a litany of trivial things like the Brady Bunch opening sequence, Carol and Paula swinging in the chuckle patch of the Magic Garden and the Pink Floyd song in which they say, "If you don't eat your meat, you can't have any pudding. How can you have any pudding if you don't eat your meat?" We've answered larger questions this way, too, from learning about our young friends in Uganda, and the struggles of paraplegics, to why silent farts stink, why knuckles crack, and how kids in other countries make musical instruments from trash. We offer honest answers about anything.

Small kids need just enough to satisfy their curiosity so your answers will vary and adapt to your children's ages.

When our daughter was about five, she saw some loose tampons in my bathroom and asked me what they were. As a doula and birth educator, the temptation was to give her all sorts of information on menstruation, why women have periods, how it allows us to have babies and so on, but I stopped myself and gave a very simple answer, "Girls have a time each month when they bleed. We're not hurt and it will happen to you when you're older, too. We use tampons to catch the blood." She nodded and walked away satisfied. I gave her an honest answer and that was all she needed.

As teens, our kids still come to us with concerns, problems, and questions. After a high school homecoming dance, our daughter came home upset and bursting with things to share. She was concerned about kids who showed up drunk and others who snuck outside, and she talked to us about it. She's come to me for help on how to handle tricky teen situations and confided in me the way a mother wants from her teen daughter. And it's not just a girl-thing. I don't believe many things are girl-traits or boy-traits, everyone's an individual. Our son, too, opens up to us about things that bother him, like the boy who pulled out a cigarette at lunch or the kid who swore at the teacher.

Naked Communication lets kids know they can trust their parents to give truthful answers. An environment of open communication helps them feel secure.

Being Open Without Giving Up Privacy or Buddying Up

In laying the groundwork for open discussions within your family, it's okay to keep some things private. Being honest does not mean sharing everything about your own teen or college years, or divulging things that are private and adult. There are things to guard and hold for yourself. There are things that are not appropriate for kids of certain ages to know or hear. If a child asks you something that is too personal, it's okay to tell them that. You can say, "I don't feel comfortable answering that right now. Maybe at some point when you're older I'll feel differently." That's still open, Naked Communication.

Honest communication also doesn't mean positioning yourself as a pal or a buddy to your child. We are not our children's peers and we shouldn't act as though we are. Recently, in a nearby town, a mother was arrested after having a houseful of teenagers to whom she was serving alcohol. She was drunk, too, when the police arrived. Parents who are trying to be cool or be buddies with their kids are not parenting.

Acting like a friend confuses children, diminishes parental authority, and blurs boundaries instead of making them clear and predictable. As parents, we treat our kids with love, respect, and cuddles but a more equal friendship doesn't evolve until they are grown, adult children and then our roles shift. Until then, be the parent.

Empowering Kids to Speak for Themselves

Notice how often you speak for your kids instead of letting them talk. Sometimes it's hard not to but work to allow and coach them to communicate for themselves. At the doctor's office, at restaurants, on play dates, and at the college admissions office, encourage your child to answer and speak for herself. Recently, at a college planning workshop with my daughter, the admissions officer spoke about her shock and dismay at how many parents call for their children. This dean of admissions wondered why their parents were handling these issues for them, if in only a few months, those kids would be living away at school on their own.

From an early age, have your children speak for themselves. You can role play with them on how to RSVP to a birthday party and then have them call the number and actually do it. There have been times that our kids couldn't find a library book or had a question at the zoo. We stand beside them if they need it, but we've had them do the asking. If they've resisted, then they don't get their book or their answer.

Usually, when we've refused to ask for them, they've braved it and gone over to do it themselves returning proud, confident and successful.

By encouraging kids to communicate their own needs and questions, you're letting them know you believe in them and they're learning self-sufficiency and independence; qualities that will serve them throughout life.

Manners Matter

Manners matter and it begins within a family. Manners are the outward way we demonstrate respect, and a close family is based on respect and courtesy. Manners are accepted rules in society that help guide people's interactions. Kids must be taught good manners as they grow. Like everything in parenting, this is not a one-time lesson. The details of general etiquette must be repeated and repeated. The parent of a toddler reminds, "Say, 'thank you,'" countless times. They repeat it until it's a habit, but manners training doesn't stop with please and thank you. There's more to it than remembering "The Magic Word."

Teach your kids good manners beyond just please and thank you, and remind them to say, "Thank you," to you, as well. After a stop for ice cream or a day at the aquarium, we would ask our children, "Can you please thank Mommy and Daddy for taking you?" Now, whenever we go out to dinner, see a movie, or do any sort of special treat, the kids always hop in the car and say, "That was fun! Thank you so much, Mom!" Manners are also about appreciating others.

Have kids write thank you notes, handwritten, mail-with-a-stamp thank you notes. Have them write notes after attending a party, receiving a gift or a special treat, and have them write notes to teachers at the end of the year and to grandparents after a weekend together. Teach kids to hold doors for others, to say excuse me, to be thoughtful and considerate, and quiet when someone is asleep.

Teach children good phone manners. We have our children answer the phone with a phrase that has resulted in many compliments of how polite they are, even from the telemarketers. They say, "Hello, this is ____, who's calling please?" Have them learn to take messages when someone calls, and how to be quiet and not interrupt when you're on the phone. If you tell them not to talk to you when you're on the phone, don't acknowledge or talk to them when they try. Set the example for your children. Our rule, only half in jest, was that unless someone was bleeding or on fire, no interrupting.

A friend of mine just shared a great way to help kids learn not to interrupt. When a child needs your attention while you're speaking to someone, the child places her hand on your shoulder. The parent acknowledges the child waiting to be heard by placing her own hand on top of her child's, then the child waits until the parent addresses her. We immediately adopted the system in our family. I love how it has the natural side effect of demonstrating social manners for our children; they observe how a parent excuses herself for a moment to attend to the child.

Model good eye contact and explain its importance to children. This is something that I believe is so critical in being a confident and successful adult. If they're talking and forgetting eye contact, we use a quiet reminder, either a silent tap on our eye or we say, "Eyes on eyes." Right along with the importance of eye contact, is the value of a strong handshake. Work with kids to hone these skills and to make the best first impression, even as youngsters.

A few summers ago, our son wanted a coveted job delivering a small local newsletter. The kids get paid in tips. He walked up to the editor, made eye contact, introduced himself and told her his interest in the job. She remembered him a whole season later, when she had openings, and sought him out commenting on how mature and polite he had been. Manners matter in life's interactions.

Good table manners and playground etiquette will make your child more pleasant to be around, and more likable through life as the playground changes to the tennis court or the board room.

Politeness is something that can often fall away in a marriage or a long-term relationship. If you've let it slide, try to bring it back into yours, your kids are watching. My husband and I thank each other, even for the things that are "our jobs" within our division of labor. It's amazing the power of saying, "Thank you for cooking dinner," "Thanks so much for taking out the garbage," or "I really appreciate you sorting through that stack of papers." Just like with children, adults, too, respond positively to positive words. The more attention you draw to the good things, the more likely those are to multiply.

Raising courteous children will make them more pleasant to be around and more well-liked by both adults and peers. It's difficult not to react, or feel negatively toward, a rude child. Yet, often, the root of discourteous behavior is that he wasn't taught well or it wasn't reinforced.

Courtesy matters when a high school senior is being interviewed for college and he doesn't make eye contact with the interviewer, it matters when a new hire is out for an important work dinner and she chews with her mouth open. Even earlier, it's important that an eight year old clears her plate at a friend's house and is able to look an adult in the eye and say, "Thank you for having me, Mrs. Fay."

These things don't appear one day when we become adults. Sure, you could pick some things up when you're older if you recognize you're missing them, but it's a parent's job to instill these respectful behaviors.

When Okay Isn't Okay

When our oldest was a toddler, I read a blurb in a parenting magazine about the one word parents shouldn't use with their children: the word *okay*.

When we tell our children to do, or not do, something, then say, "Okay?" it implies that we are seeking their input or opening an invitation to discussion. If we say, "Johnny, come here," it is much more effective than, "Johnny, come here, okay?" The simple okay gives Johnny a choice we never intended to give him.

In communicating with children, from very young ages, we cannot be ambiguous. We need to be succinct and specific. We're much more likely to get the results we're after (good listening is on every parent's wish list) if we deliver a clear directive: "Do not touch the glass." Even a pre-walker can understand what his parent wants. He may test you, but repeating the same, concise message with a gentle removal of his hand will teach him that you mean what you say without question. See Naked Discipline.

I think what is really meant in a parent's mind when adding okay is, "Did you understand me?" or "Got it?" but instead, using okay makes instructions much less definitive and diminishes your parental authority.

A direction stated this way, "Please put your shoes in the basket, okay?" isn't really a direction at all, it's a suggestion; it grants a child the option to *not* do what you asked.

Remove the okay and say it out loud, "Please put your shoes in the basket." Does it sound stronger and more certain? There is no longer any doubt to the child what you want her to do, it's much more likely to be productive.

I hear parents adding "okay" all the time in daily life, at the grocery store, playground or library: "You can't have that, okay?" "Time to go, okay?" "Only five books, okay?" It becomes a habitual word, used without thought or mindfulness, and it strips a parent of his/her control and charge of the situation. "Okay?" is asking for consensus or approval when we really don't mean to give the child an opinion or choice.

As confident parents, we're in charge. We can be in charge in a loving, nurturing way, but we're the parents and we're not giving suggestions or recommendations, we are actually giving orders. It may sound harsh to some, but as parents, we want our children to do what we say, to listen to us, and to do what they're told, when they're told. This builds a foundation of not only respect for others, but of self-respect, as well, and kids learn early the relationship between their actions and resulting outcomes.

We're guiding and teaching and shaping our kids' interactions with the world. Having children who do what they're told is also a matter of safety. If a child is running into the parking lot, we'd yell, "STOP!" not "STOP, okay?" There's no choice. So why say, "Don't touch that plug, okay?"

Kids feel more secure and settled knowing what is expected of them and in receiving clear limits, boundaries, and communication from their parents. If you think you may be a parent who uses "okay" a lot, try it for a day – or take a one week challenge. Stop ending sentences with "okay?" and instead aim to articulate what you want of your child.

Don't Use Baby Talk

Once your babies aren't babies, speak to them as you would an adult. Our oldest two kids, both teenagers, recently had an interaction with an adult who spoke to them as if they were babies. Her high-pitched tone and lilting voice made them feel uncomfortable and disrespected. They felt like she didn't understand them and like she thought they were dumb. Are those the feelings you want to stir in your kids? Speak to your kids intelligently, if they don't get something, they'll ask.

On a similar note, call kids by their name. Decades ago in New York City, I worked with a woman who always referred to her daughter as "the baby," I was surprised when I finally learned that "the baby" was two years old. I've wondered how them calling her that changed their expectations and interactions with her, and how that influenced how she grew up. Using a child's name is reassuring and validating.

Do Use Humor

Our son is brilliant at making his sisters laugh, and he can pull them, or his parents, right out of a funk. He sets a great example for us in his use of humor.

When the kids were toddlers, a fail-proof trick was to calmly and seriously tell a grumpy child, "Don't laugh," and the smiles and giggles poured out. It worked every time. Older kids and teens become a little harder, but it's still a valuable tip to remember that humor can change the tone of a moment. Used with wise timing, laughter can shift a tense or escalating conflict to a more positive interaction. Laughing calms us, connects us and relaxes us, which are all valuable for changing the mood and redirecting the conversation to be more productive.

More Naked Communication

Naked Communication increases children's confidence, independence and self-assurance. Through open communication, kids know they can come to you for honest answers and they know you respect their questions and won't laugh at them. They feel secure in being able to talk with you, and know that you're there to guide them, about things they don't understand or that frighten them.

If kids know they can communicate honestly with you, they're more likely to call you for help in a tough situation. The son of a friend of ours was at that party where the mother was drunk and serving the teens alcohol. When he saw what was going on, he texted his father to come get him which demonstrated his security in that relationship, and in the ability to freely communicate with his parents.

Learning communication skills and manners will help kids to be better received by others and more able to achieve what they set out to do in life. It wouldn't go over so well to slurp soup in a lunch meeting or to look down at your lap through an interview. It's our job as parents to teach and model good communication and manners to our kids.

Naked Communication Top Tips:

- Be clear and transparent about your expectations.

- Kids need to be able to anticipate cause and effect.

- Children should know they can get honest answers from their parents about anything.

- Questions are opportunities to share values and beliefs.

- Kids need just enough to satisfy their curiosity. Vary and adapt answers to your children's ages.

- It's okay to keep some things private.

- Honest communication doesn't mean positioning yourself as a pal to your child.

- Encourage your child to answer and speak for herself.

- Teach good manners, eye contact and model politeness.

- Don't add, "okay?" to the end of your sentences.

- Speak to your kids intelligently, don't use baby talk.

Children are natural mimics who act like their parents despite every effort to teach them good manners.
- Author Unknown

Children have more need of models than of critics.
- Carolyn Coats,
Things Your Dad Always Told You
But You Didn't Want to Hear

Chapter 5

Naked Responsibility

Personal Responsibility

Taking responsibility for our own actions is not always easy, but it's an essential life skill. Teaching a child who spilled her juice to help clean it up is helping her take charge of her own accident. It's quicker for us to just do it, but then we've wiped away the lessons with the spill.

Having a child write an apology note to the babysitter for being difficult at bedtime is having him acknowledge that he alone controls his actions, that he made a bad choice, and that he needs to make it better.

Teach children that no one else makes you act a certain way. Things will always come at you in life, but it's all about how you respond and what attitude you choose to take. Attitude is everything. The favorite, well-known poem

"Attitude" by Charles Swindol hangs near our kitchen table, and if someone needs an attitude nudge, we pull it out for them to read aloud to the family.

Every moment in every day we all have choices. There's a tendency to point a finger away from ourselves as the cause of our misery or mistake, but we can reframe that for children and help them to understand the necessity in taking responsibility for one's own actions and one's own happiness.

For example, a child who misses an assignment might say, "I didn't know about it, the teacher never told us it was due," or other such excuses. It's a parent's job to help the child recognize that the missing assignment is not the teacher's fault but the child's, and then brainstorm ways to solve the problem. Kids need to learn that they must first identify a problem before they can change or correct it. The first step is taking responsibility for the problem. As parents, we can walk them through this learning process.

Help kids understand that we all mess up sometimes but it's how we handle it that matters. Politics offers many good examples on taking, or not taking, personal responsibility. For older kids, if you follow politics, you can point out the stories of people denying an act, running away from it, and lying about it versus those who step up at the outset, saying they did the bad thing, apologizing and resigning, or taking actions to make it better. Giving kids real life examples, from the news or the neighborhood, illustrates the value of taking personal responsibility.

Personal responsibility applies to every area of life. School is a child's job. They must have integrity, and be dependable with their projects, studying and assignments. Kids earn the grades they get. Whether it's an A or a C, we must help them to correlate their actions and behaviors to the outcome on the report card. The teacher didn't "give" them any grade, the student earned it for better or for worse.

It's empowering for kids to take a question about a grade or an assignment directly to the teacher. As a parent, when kids are in upper elementary school and older, unless there is a bullying or larger issue, encourage your kids to talk for themselves. The student should talk to the teacher and arrange a make-up test for the day of an absence, the kid should be the one to tell them she messed up or forgot something and ask if she can still get credit for turning it in late. It's not easy, but again, the hard thing is often the right thing.

Personal responsibility is fostered in the question: Who cares? Parents should ask themselves who cares about the kids' grades or messy bedroom or anything else, then determine if it is the parent or the child who cares more. Then, make it the child who cares more. As parents, we're not shirking our responsibility to guide and teach them, but we can structure things so that it's the kid who has the greater stake in it.

For example, we have a messy bedroom problem in our house (to be fair, it's the teenagers, not our youngest, usually). I was always ranting and taking away phones or computer time and bugging them all weekend until it was done, or kind of done. What finally changed was when I realized that I cared more about their clean bedrooms than they did. Ah Ha! So now if their rooms aren't clean (my standard of clean, not theirs) after school each day, they lose activities and playing outside for the rest of the day. Now who cares if their rooms are clean? For this to be effective, be honest in your actions and follow through. For younger kids, if they make a good-faith effort to do what you want, that counts.

It comes down to control. We need to provide kids with opportunities to find motivation, and desire to be responsible, *within* themselves. They need to make that shift from "things are being done to me" to "I'm able to affect change." No adult with a victim mentality is happy and we don't want that for our children. Never let your kids get away with blaming others for their actions, their mood, or their position in life.

Chores and Responsibilities

Responsibility for children's possessions is an area ripe

for learning. Taking care of the things and space around you shows respect. It stinks when a child loses a favorite toy or breaks a special game, but my husband and I have never believed in running out to replace it. Instead, we've discussed with the child how it happened, how it could've been avoided, and brainstormed ideas for finding it or saving the child's own money to buy a new one.

Having kids save their own money to buy a desired item from their allowance, birthday gifts, or odd jobs is the best way to teach them responsibility. The purchases our kids have made with their own money are always exceptionally well cared for and appreciated.

Once, our kids came home telling me that their friend had left his handheld gaming device outside overnight and it had rained. It didn't work anymore. What the kids were amazed at was that his parents went out and bought him a new one. The kids said, "You wouldn't do that!" It wasn't said accusatorially or wishfully, it was said gratefully. They understood that it was the child's responsibility and were meaning, "You wouldn't go out and get us a new toy after we were irresponsible, didn't take care of it, and let it get broken." Proud Mama Moment! They GOT IT!

Giving kids jobs around the house teaches them about the value of sharing the housework, about the efforts that go into running a household (a tiny little glimpse), and it's another way to teach responsibility. Having household tasks they need to complete between homework and activities isn't always easy, but it's a smart life lesson and a cornerstone of Naked Responsibility.

Some ideas on how to manage chores:

- Use checklists, one for each kid

- Jobs can change weekly, monthly or daily

- Some jobs can always be one child's job, something they can take total ownership of

- To rotate the list of jobs, use clothes pins labeled with each child's name and pin cards with a group of tasks to each

- Write jobs on wide popsicle sticks and have them choose a stick and do that job

- Make a sign-up list of tasks, with the pay for each listed, and have the kids sign up

Our kids receive payment for certain jobs on their list, (see the Stone Reward System in Naked Discipline) and there are other things they are expected to pitch in and do, just because it's the right thing to do as part of a family.

Start having kids help out young. Even small children can be expected to pick up their toys, put shoes in a basket, set the table, empty wastebaskets, unload silverware from the dishwasher, carry out recycling, or help wash vegetables for dinner. You can also include daily expectations on your lists. Adding things like hanging up a backpack, practicing piano, and being on time for the bus can help build good habits.

In chores and in life, our family has a no complaining policy. If kids argue or moan about doing a job, they will still be required to do it, but they will lose some of the pay with each complaint. In our house, laziness earns extra jobs. Grumble and you'll end up with more work and less pay. That policy has helped limit (though there are still plenty of occasions for reminders) complaining about doing household work.

Goal Setting

Goal setting is a life skill and a gift to teach kids young. I love the Napoleon Hill quote, "A goal is a dream with a deadline," we can dream, but we need to quantify it to help us achieve it.

Teaching and modeling goal setting encourages kids to strive in life. It's putting action behind the words: "You can do anything you set your mind to," or "You can be anything you want to be." Teaching kids how to set goals, and map out mini-goals along the path, is giving them the tools to really be anything they want to be.

Effective goal setting includes writing it down. Good, old-fashioned pen and paper. You can have your kids illustrate the goal or cut out magazine pictures and make a collage around their written goal. Hang it somewhere prominent, above their bed, beside the bathroom mirror, somewhere they can see it during daily tasks.

The goals need to be specific and quantifiable. For example, you could guide a child whose goal is "to be a better reader" to create a goal like, "I will be a better reader and will move to the next reading level by the end of the school year." That is a measurable and achievable target.

Next, help them plan steps they can take daily and weekly to work toward the bigger goal. If a child's written goal was to "get straight A's on my next quarter report card," the daily and weekly action steps could include completing daily homework, handing assignments in on time, and studying notes each night. It's the everyday work that builds toward positive life habits and deliberately drives us toward our bigger vision.

In the bonus material at the end of this book, you'll find a simple Naked Parenting Goal Form to help kids with goal setting. At the dinner table, we talk about each kid's goal for the month and help each other formulate the daily and weekly steps to get there. The "debriefing" and discussions at the end of the month address the process of achieving the goal and become equally, or more, valuable than the goal itself. This can also be used in January to lay out longer term goals for the year.

Even if a goal isn't achieved on time or completely, by doing this exercise, by setting intentions, and being accountable, even just within your family, your kids (and you) will be closer to accomplishing that goal than they would've been without having put the energy and focus on it. It gives them confidence in their ability to make a positive difference through their own actions and continues to build skills for lifelong satisfaction and success.

Falling short of a goal teaches many life lessons in itself. Working through feelings like regret, disappointment, and setbacks in a loving, nurturing setting can help kids to manage those Naked Emotions as they grow up and can also serve to be a strong motivator.

Goal setting is a life skill, a self-improvement tool, a means of self-reflection, self-discipline, and taking personal responsibility. There is so much that kids are learning on the way toward their goals that getting there is only part of the victory.

More Naked Responsibility

Personal responsibility begins at home. Hold kids

responsible for their actions. Give them jobs around the house so you can encourage them to save, give, and buy things they want. Teach kids that their success or failure is not determined by outside factors, but that they are in charge of their actions and that their success or failure is within their control. Naked Responsibility teaches kids confidence. Kids who make the connection between positive or negative consequences and their own actions feel more secure, can navigate life better, and make better choices. When kids feel responsible and confident, they are more likely, and able, to reach out and help others.

In helping others, kids become examples for those around them. Kindness and serving other people encompass many of the main principles of Naked Parenting, including love, gratitude, emotional honesty, and empathy.

Naked Responsibility Top Tips:

- Attitude is everything.

- Every moment in every day you have choices. How will you respond?

- Help kids understand that we all mess up sometimes, but it's in how we handle it that matters.

- Personal responsibility applies to every area of life.

- Who cares? As parents, we need to make it the child who cares more than us.

- Help kids make that shift from "things are being done to me" to "I'm able to affect change."

- Teach kids responsibility for their own possessions.

- Have kids save their own money to buy a desired item.

- Start kids helping out with jobs around the house when they're young.

- Teaching and modeling goal setting to kids is setting them up to strive in life.

- Falling short of a goal teaches many life lessons in itself.

- Never let your kids get away with blaming others for their actions, their mood, or their position in life.

- Teach kids that they are in charge of their actions and their own success or failure is within their control.

If you want children to keep their feet on the ground, put some responsibility on their shoulders.
- Abigail Van Buren

The greater danger for most of us lies not in setting our aim too high and falling short; but in setting our aim too low, and achieving our mark.
- Michelangelo Buonarroti

Chapter 6

Naked Discipline

Disciplining our kids is not easy. It's exhausting and frustrating, but it's intrinsic in our job as parents. Disciplining our kids can create feelings of sadness, guilt, anger, impatience and helplessness in the best of parents, but that's no reason not to take charge and do it.

Discipline has two sides – negative consequences for undesirable behaviors and positive consequences for good behaviors. It's one of the fun parts of parenting to reward our kids' good choices in life. Praising and acknowledging the behaviors you want to encourage is the best way to influence and guide your child. However, kids do misbehave and, in working with parents and being a parent, it's dealing with the not-listening, the rule-breaking behaviors that's so challenging.

Disciplining is Teaching - Disciplining is Necessary

As parents, it's our job to keep our kids safe, to set limits for them, to communicate those limits and to give reasonable and swift consequences when kids break a rule or don't listen.

The point is learning. Discipline is all about teaching our children how to behave and interact with the world, beginning at home. Kids need, and thrive, with firm boundaries and it's our job to set them.

It can be uncomfortable, and flat out not fun, to execute time outs or to take away a fun event. It requires endless energy to mold kids' behaviors, to determine adequate consequences, then to stick it out and deliver them in a timely way. Since our goal is teaching, it's necessary to follow through on a logical consequence right away so children connect the discomfort with the undesirable behavior.

Knowing exactly what motivates a child offers a perfect immediate consequence but that can punish the parent, too, and that's where wavering can seep in. A long car ride without a gadget may be tough, but if it's educating our child on the importance of proper conduct, well, then as the parent, we need to see it through however hard it is on us.

Another option is to present a child with two consequences from which they can choose. I feel this method is more effective with older children and by giving them limited control during the process, it can help them to better accept the consequence. When kids absorb the consequence as being a result of their own actions, instead of seeing it as a parent doing something to them, they are more likely to learn from it.

Also, as they get older, you can ask your child to think about their actions and then return to you with several ideas for consequences. Often, they will suggest things that are more severe than you would have designed. Discuss it together and decide upon a reasonable, fair, and teachable consequence for the offending behavior.

Using fines for older children can be very effective, as well. It fits the requirement of being a swift, meaningful action. One way we've used fines is if the kids miss the bus. They are expected to be up in time to get ready and out the door on time with all of their required materials for the day, and if they need a ride to school, it inconveniences the parent who drives them, perhaps even making them late for work or an appointment. Therefore, in our house, if a child misses the bus, the first time it's a warning, the second time it costs them $1 for the ride, the next time it costs them $2, paid up front before they get in the car to go to school. How often do you think they miss the bus? At the beginning of last year, we got to $5 with our son, then he made it to the bus the rest of the year.

Whether in a time-out, or losing a chance to go to the movies, it's difficult to see our kids upset and/or crying, but we're the adults and need to bear that discomfort and manage our own feelings. We need to be the grown-ups and carry that weight for the long term good of our children. Saying, "No," does not mean "I don't love you." In many ways, saying, "No," can mean, "I love you very much so I'm exerting the effort to teach you this."

Parents are so often afraid that their children won't love them if they give time-outs or consequences for their actions, but with Naked Love, for kids who know they are loved unconditionally, this is not the case.

Through the years, our kids have grumbled, stormed out or cried throughout an earned consequence while my stomach twisted, my heart knotted, and my head ached. I've cried privately as they banged on the floor in anger, and steeled myself to stick it out, as awful as it was. I've had to be more stubborn than the child who got out of a time-out 38 times until he served his time and understood I meant it. More times than I can count, when they've returned to me after calming, and after serving out the consequence, all on their own, they've given me a hug and said, "I'm sorry," and "I love you, Mommy."

It's so important to reconnect after a tousle but as tough

as it is, it's critical to see through that tousle in the first place. Kids are resilient and will love you and respect you, even more over time, for setting and enforcing your family limits.

If we back down from seeing a consequence through to relieve our own uncomfortable emotions, we are ineffective in parenting. We have only taught our children that they can cry, fuss or tantrum their way out of a sanction. They have not learned to choose the appropriate behavior, and the next time, it will be exponentially harder for that parent.

In "rescuing" a child after we've given a consequence because we feel guilty or unhappy, we transfer difficult feelings to our child. They experience uncertainty and imbalance from inconsistent messages and a lack of boundaries.

We must follow through and do what we say we'll do if a rule is breached. Leave the playdate if you've threatened, "The next time you grab a toy, we're leaving!" Pick your child up and leave if that's what you warned would happen.

Years ago, when our son was around four, we had been looking forward to our annual strawberry picking trip. I haven't the vaguest idea what offense he committed but he had received a warning and I told him that if he did it again, he would not come strawberry picking. Well, you know what happened. He did it again.

Inside, I was miserable, I wanted him to come. Instead, now I had to call and pay for a babysitter that I really shouldn't have needed. My heart felt sad that he would miss out on a fun family tradition in its infancy and I was angry that he didn't just listen. I found a sitter, said good-bye and my daughters and I left the house. It was tough. Really tough.

All these years later, he still remembers that he missed out on strawberry picking. He doesn't remember why either, but the lesson he learned is that Mom will do what she says she will do. He learned that he needs to listen or he'll miss out on something he cares about, and those are meaningful messages. Taking away one strawberry farm trip paid off in significant ways.

So do you have to discipline by taking away birthday parties or a trip to the ice cream shop? No. Every kid is different and many might never need that; some children will respond well to a firm voice or a stern look. But here's the key: If you don't want to take it away, don't say you will. If you say you'll take it away, then you must follow through.

Each time a child connects his naughty behavior with a negative consequence that is age-appropriate and delivered quickly, that experience builds upon the last. Nothing happens overnight so consistency matters. Consistency is that 100% true term that is always associated with disciplining and parenting. Consistency matters.

Disciplining our kids doesn't have to be negative. Deliver your consequence calmly and steadily. I always find I'm most effective when I simply state the problem, state the consequence and then do it. Of course, we're human and yelling or droning on and on sometimes happens, but when I stick to the brief message, it always works better. Clearly, a model of control is preferable to a screaming, blabbing lunatic.

In the heat of those moments, it's common for parents to have mixed and conflicting feelings. Arm yourself by thinking and planning ahead. What are the key behaviors you're trying to work on in your home right now? Pick the top one or two to focus on for the next month. Assign specific consequences to each infraction and write them down for yourself, if you need to, for reference. Written outcomes for certain behaviors can be helpful for older children, too, and provide another way to openly communicate your expectations. Kids must be able to predict what the result of their actions will be.

Next, communicate succinctly and definitively to your child: 1. What you expect. 2. What will happen if they don't do what you expect. And then, do it.

The Stone Reward System

Reward systems are often useful in motivating and disciplining kids, a task which requires endless parental creativity and energy. It's a powerful technique, too, at times, to offer praise to a child in front of others. Many times, a parent's compliment or approval are all the positive reinforcement and reward a child needs, but here's one idea that has worked well for our family in addition to verbal acknowledgment.

Our family's stone reward system started very simply years ago, and over time, it has been reinvented and continues to be an effective parenting tool.

We started with a package of smooth stones from the craft store and three clear tumbler-sized votive candle holders. Having a translucent jar helps the kids to see their progress and letting them select the stones is an easy way to get them instantly involved and on board when you unveil the new plan. When we caught a kiddo doing something worth rewarding, they got to put a stone in their jar.

Listening the first time, getting ready for school on time, making their bed, or helping their sister, all earned a stone. The new system forced my husband and me to look for the good in the kids and to focus on the behaviors we wanted to encourage instead of ranting about those that caused us frustration.

A positive offshoot started to bloom. As soon as we rewarded a stone to one child, the others were immediately aware of their actions and altered them to work toward earning a stone, too. Eventually, we instated a "no-ask" policy, the kids couldn't do something nice then ask for a stone, it needed to be awarded not requested. Another heartwarming, unanticipated side effect was that the kids started to tell us about the good deeds of their siblings, for example, "Mom, Anna deserves a stone, she just helped me clean my room."

When they filled their jar, they would receive a larger reward which they selected ahead. The goal reward doesn't have to cost anything, you can decide what genre of rewards works for you. Some ideas are a special hike alone with one parent, a book or small toy, a night out for ice cream or the privilege of choosing a special dinner or dessert.

After a while, the stone system in its original format slowed down and needed revamping. The kids were older and had new interests, so each earned stone counted for five minutes of computer or TV time; no stones, no computer. We also put some restrictions on how many stones they could use at one time or in one day. You can adapt this to fit your family's values. It worked so well that our youngest learned her five's times tables very young as she counted out six stones to watch 30 minutes of TV.

Eventually that system wore itself out, too, and money had become increasingly more valuable to the kids, so we merged the stones with household chores. When the kids do their list of jobs they are paid in stones, each one worth $0.25, and then we pay them at the end of the month. No work = no stone = no money.

We still have them throw in some stones for kind acts, prompt listening and self-motivation. I love rewarding them with extra stones when they do something without me needing to remind them or when they happily volunteer to do a task.

The stones can also be the perfect solution as a consequence for undesirable behavior. Discipline must be done in a timely way with a loss of privilege or an immediate consequence that fits the offense. Sometimes the hardest part of this is finding the exact right consequence for the act. There are times when something needs an acknowledgement that it was wrong or unacceptable, but a grand penalty isn't warranted. I find that asking them to take out a stone for a specific reason is very effective. They care about their stones and it's meaningful to them to lose one.

Make it your own, get creative with jars, colored stones, try different containers for each child or color-coded stones. Start out with a set of guidelines for your reward system and work with it, give it a chance, but be open and willing to sit as a family and change it up if it no longer serves its purpose. Get the kids involved in brainstorming the details.

Check the bonus material at the end of the book for using paper chains to motivate and reward kids.

More Naked Discipline

Discipline can be uncomfortable and unpleasant for parents, but it's our job to deal with difficult emotions in ourselves in order to teach our children. It hurts to feel our kid's raw pain, but we must allow them to feel sad, angry, or remorseful instead of rescuing them. It's the hard thing but the right thing.

If we can't manage to accept and cope with tough feelings, how can we expect our kids to do that? Disciplining kids can create feelings of guilt or other negative emotions in a parent, but we must, as the adult, deal with our feelings to benefit our children.

Naked Discipline increases children's confidence because they know their limits and can feel safe exploring. Kids will always push against the limits to test them, but the more firm those boundaries stay, the more secure a child can feel. Kids thrive with parents confidently in charge and lovingly enforcing limits. They can grow and step out into the world because they have clear expectations and an understanding that their actions have consequences, both positive and negative.

Naked Discipline Top Tips:

- Disciplining our kids is not easy, but it's a necessary part of the job.

- Discipline is about teaching our children how to behave and interact with the world.

- It's difficult to see our kids crying and upset, but we're the adults and need to bear that discomfort and manage our own feelings.

- Saying, "No," does not mean "I don't love you."

- If we back down to relieve our own uncomfortable emotions, we are ineffective in parenting.

- If you don't want to take it away, don't say you will. If you say you'll take it away, then follow through.

- Reward systems are often useful in motivating and disciplining kids.

- Kids thrive with parents confidently in charge and lovingly enforcing limits.

Don't handicap your children by making their lives easy.
- Robert A. Heinlein

Parents who are afraid to put their foot down usually have children who step on their toes.
- Chinese Proverb

73

Chapter 7

Naked Mistakes

Apologize

Ah, mistakes. Let's talk first about ours. There are times when we screw up and it's appropriate to apologize to our kids. Sitting them down to explain our mess-up gives our children front rows seats in taking personal responsibility. It reinforces your respect for them and is another way to teach empathy allowing them to see their parents as humans who make mistakes and have feelings, too.

So when you recognize you've made a whopper, model what we'd expect from our kids: identify it, own it and make it better. If you find yourself needing to say you're sorry frequently, it's time to go back to Naked Emotions and do some self-examination, take responsibility, and adjust your actions to get different results. Remember, as parents, we set the tone in our home.

Be kind to yourself and don't let guilt get in your way. It's a fact of life that we make mistakes, it's all in how we handle them that matters. Do your best, aim to do something today to make yourself a little better than yesterday, and keep loving those kiddos. Being a confident parent will serve your kids well.

Mistakes and Failures as Opportunities

Family meetings are a great tool to address a negative trend in the house, to initiate a new system of expectations, or to work together to problem solve. After a tough day or a string of difficult behavior, it's helpful to gather the family, or sometimes just the main offender and both parents if possible, and have a chat. These talks should use the principles of Naked Communication, and be loving, open, and done at a time when everyone is calm, not in the heat of the moment.

Discuss a troubling behavior and ask the child to take responsibility for it, speaking aloud will help a child integrate the cause and effect of her actions. Work together to list possible solutions, ways to prevent or handle a similar problem in the future, and to talk about what was learned. Once the child has taken ownership and taken action to rectify the situation as agreed upon, hug her, tell her how proud you are of how responsible she's being then move on without dwelling or harping on the problem.

Use mistakes, yours and your children's, as opportunities to learn, grow and improve. Failures and losses, while painful at the time, can become valuable opportunities. Your kids will struggle through not making the team, not getting the lead in the play, or losing the big game. In the immediate aftermath, it's important to validate their feelings and not diminish them. There will be a time to reframe the loss, to help them learn from it, but in the moment of loss, allow kids, even encourage them, to go ahead and feel sad, angry, upset, disappointed, and frustrated. Don't rescue them from these tough feelings and don't diminish them or brush them off.

My brother used to have a framed picture in his bedroom growing up that said, "The problem with being a good sport is you have to lose to prove it." Of course, that's not really true and good sportsmanship is shown in winning as well as losing, but it speaks to how no one likes to lose. In life, mistakes, losses and failures help us to grow and improve, even though they can stink and hurt at the time.

Mistakes Motivate

With a baby trying to crawl, a toddler working on a puzzle, or a teen struggling to learn a difficult piece of music, frustration propels learning. The feeling of frustration pushes us and drives us forward to achievement. Don't rob your child of the accomplishment, of the success after the hard work, because you don't want him to feel frustrated. Let him feel the tough emotions, stand beside him to support him and love him, but he must go right through the crummy stuff to get to the good stuff.

Children who feel proficient and successful in many areas will feel more successful throughout their life. This directly builds his confidence. To become competent and excel, it takes practice, opportunity, varied experiences and it also takes mistakes. No one becomes great at anything without some bumps along the way.

Finding the lessons in mistakes, and letting kids manage their errors, will help them as they age and the stakes for their missteps increase. How well is a kid going to fare when he's away at college for the first time if he's never been allowed to fail, always been rescued and had things "fixed" for him? What happens when that kid misses a deadline, gets a girl pregnant or gets behind a wheel after drinking? Good sense doesn't just happen. We learn, like all else, little by little, throughout life. Don't cushion their paths, instead be there to guide and love them through the tough times.

We shouldn't engineer childhood so that our kids don't experience failures. Our aim is to help them grow from the smaller mistakes of childhood so that as they get older, they're less apt to make life-altering, serious-impact mistakes.

Kids learn resiliency from Naked Mistakes because they believe they can bounce back from set-backs in life. Having learned personal responsibility, and that they are in control of their successes and failures, they will be more confident as they get back up and try again. Help kids to learn to persist despite, and in spite of, mistakes and failures.

Naked Mistakes Top Tips:

- There are times when we screw up and it's appropriate to apologize to our kids.

- It's a fact of life that we make mistakes, it's all in how we handle them that matters.

- Family meetings are a great tool. Use the principles of Naked Communication.

- Use mistakes, yours and your children's, as opportunities to learn, grow and improve.

- Validate kids' feelings. Encourage kids to feel sad, angry, upset, disappointed, and frustrated.

- Don't rescue kids from tough feelings and don't diminish them.

- In life, mistakes, loses and failures help us to grow and improve.

- The more areas in which a child can feel proficient and successful, the better for him throughout life. This directly builds his confidence.

- Don't cushion kids' paths, instead be there to guide and love them through the tough times.

- Kids learn resiliency from Naked Mistakes because they believe they can bounce back from set-backs in life.

You may make mistakes, but you are not a failure until you start blaming someone else.

- Mary Pickford

Nothing in the world can take the place of persistence. Talent will not; nothing is more common than unsuccessful men with talent. Genius will not; unrewarded genius is almost a proverb. Education will not; the world is full of educated derelicts. Persistence and determination alone are omnipotent. The slogan Press On! has solved and always will solve the problems of the human race.

- Calvin Coolidge

Chapter 8

Naked Gratitude

To me, gratitude wraps it all up. I believe that the key to happiness is in being grateful. If we're able to model and to teach kids to be thankful for what they have right now, in this moment, we foster contentment and joy. Being grateful doesn't mean we don't strive for more out of life or reach toward dreams and goals, but it gives us peace on the journey.

Living Gratefully

I strive to live gratefully every day. It's an active process, one that takes regular reminding and effort, but it's gratitude, I believe, that is the key to happiness. My whole life, my grandmother's mantra was, "Count your blessings," she embodied this philosophy and truly lived with gratitude. I work to practice gratitude with a daily gratitude journal and through conscious choice and deliberate effort. Gratitude is a gift of peace and happiness to myself, and by extrapolation, to my family and those around me.

If I can be grateful for where I am in this exact point in time, at this place in my life, if I can be thankful for the love around me right now, well, then I believe I've found the secret to life.

By living gratefully and modeling this for kids, we can help combat the entitlement mentality of many youth. In homes with plenty, within a nation of plenty, it's a struggle to help kids see how truly great they have it. Lessons in gratitude make a difference.

Teaching Kids Gratitude

One tool we use to teach our kids to be grateful is to go around the table at dinner each night and everyone shares a high point of their day. Often our best moments are small things and the activity focuses us on the good.

We also have a no complaining policy. Complaining is all about the negative and it can be the grown-up equivalent of whining. No one wants to be around or hear from a complainer. This goes straight back to Naked Responsibility and taking charge of one's situation, and if you don't like where you are, change things or choose to focus on being grateful for what you have. Empowering kids in this way lays the groundwork for a life of looking for opportunities and positives instead of moaning about something not going their way. It takes consistency and reminders to make this a habit.

Recently, my sister got my daughter tickets to a concert in Boston and we each brought a friend. Leading up to the date, she had been really excited about the evening and the show. As the four of us strolled the cobbled streets of Quincy Market and Faneuil Hall, the wind whipped us and we pulled our coats tighter, but then my daughter started complaining. Not just about the cold, but she rattled off a few other things, too, she was hungry, her feet hurt, I don't remember the list, but I gave her a solid mother's-stare and mouthed, "No complaining." She realized her error and how ungrateful she sounded on a really special night and stopped immediately.

Recognizing how good we have it isn't always easy, but shifting to gratitude always feels better. Humans have a "negativity bias" so it can take some conscious effort to keep refocusing on the positives, but it can become a habit and it's a habit worth making. It will be exponentially harder for kids to live gratefully if their parents aren't modeling the way for them.

The Family Budget

This subject loops us back to Naked Communication as well as Naked Responsibility. Everyone has different feelings on discussing finances with children, but in the philosophy of Naked Parenting, I believe kids should be let in on aspects of the family finances at age-appropriate levels. It gives kids perspective and understanding on the value of money and what things around them cost. It can be an entree into lessons on money management, saving, investing, business ideas or getting a job babysitting or lawn mowing.

Speaking to kids about finances also teaches them to be grateful and to appreciate what they have. Let them see the bills for the activities in which they participate. Do they know the cost of the uniform, the cleats, the guitar teacher, the swimming class? Including them in these issues fosters responsibility and will help in their decision-making. Maybe they don't really like gymnastics enough for mom and dad to be spending all that money on classes, meets and leotards. You may be surprised by how young a child can be to use this information in making decisions if given the opportunity.

One idea is to allocate a certain budget for activities for each child and let them decide how they chose to spend their activity allowance. We've used a clothing allowance in the past, as my mom did with me. When teens want new clothes but have no concept of the expense of it, it's a real eye-opener to give them a set sum of money that they must manage for any clothing needs for six months, for example. If she needs socks or new sneakers, she has to be sure not to spend the whole thing on graphic T-s on a trip to the mall. Spending decisions change dramatically when kids have control and a stake in things.

A few times, while out at a restaurant, when the bill came, we asked each kid to guess the total amount of our dinner. Of course, they were all off by *a lot* and were shocked to learn what a dinner out for five people really costs. Appreciation dawned on their faces and sincere, "Thank yous," followed. This is an exercise and teaching tool to give the kids a sense of perspective, never to cause guilt or worry.

Another strategy is to give a child an amount that fits your family's budget and ask them to plan a fun family day with that money. Have them research museums, restaurants, hiking trails and whatever it is they plan, then have them write up a budget for the allocated funds. Then, let them manage the money for the day they planned, giving them lessons in, among other things, speaking up for themselves as they buy tickets or make reservations and being a leader within the family.

These tools help kids appreciate what they have, begin to understand the value of money and the things around them, and to be grateful for their stuff and their activities.

Family Traditions and Rituals

Traditions and rituals strengthen family bonds and give us a sense of security, belonging and shared identity. They give us structure and organize the world around us and they can teach us cultural and religious heritages as well as family values and beliefs. Rituals are vital during times of change and upheaval providing comfort and a better ability to cope. Family traditions give us lifelong memories and a special way to stay connected with our past. The predictability, the comfort of daily, monthly or yearly rituals, unites family members, even across generations.

Every year, when we dye Easter eggs, I still make an egg that is pink with yellow spots. I'd written a story in second grade about that egg so I made one every year. My sister sends me pictures, and I can hear her laughing, because when she dyes eggs, she makes one, too. Now my kids will often beat me to it, knowing we have to have a pink egg with yellow spots. It's a silly, little thing, with a thread that binds us.

Daily rituals like prioritizing family dinners, singing bedtime songs, or snuggling with a child before starting the morning are all valuable practices that nurture everyone in the family. Rituals can be for the whole family or can be special for only a few members. My dad used to take me out to breakfast as a special treat, it was just the two of us and it's a treasured memory.

When our oldest was a baby, we began the tradition of taking a fresh cut from our Christmas tree and writing the date and a special memory of that year's celebration on the wedge. We now have a basket full of tree trunks and it's a wonderful time each year when we pull them out and read them. Each kid's first Christmas and moves to new homes are represented, the years we added nephews to the family, lost a grandparent, or had two feet of snow are recorded.

Include traditions of gratitude in your family. Ideas are a family gratitude jar where everyone writes things they're thankful for and adds the slips of paper to the jar, a special gratitude box or put them into a photo album to create a gratitude book. Make it a tradition to write thank you notes to our troops overseas, serve at a local food pantry or soup kitchen, or join an annual spring cleaning at a local park.

Continue traditions from your childhood and create new ones. Cherish the value of rituals within the family and use them to problem solve, to impart your family culture and beliefs, and to model the lessons you want to share with your children.

Naked Gratitude Top Tips:

- The key to happiness is in being grateful.

- Have a family no-complaining policy.

- Recognizing how good we have it isn't always easy, but shifting to gratitude always feels better.

- Let kids in on aspects of the family finances at age-appropriate levels.

- Sharing financial information gives kids perspective and understanding on the value of money.

- Let kids see the bills for the activities in which they participate.

- Use tools to help kids appreciate what they have and the value of money.

- Traditions and rituals strengthen family bonds and give a sense of security, belonging and shared identity.

- Continue traditions from your childhood and create new ones.

Gratitude is not only the greatest of virtues, but the parent of all others.
- Cicero

Each day of our lives we make deposits in the memory banks of our children.
- Charles R. Swindoll

Conclusion

You're already a good parent. Naked or not. It's important to keep growing, learning and seeking new ideas and information as parents, and by reading this book, I hope you've added to your skills and creative reserves. I hope you're now able to try out the concepts and examples presented here and to feel more confident and satisfied as a parent.

You've seen how the principles and skills of Naked Parenting interrelate and build upon one another. As you add nakedness to your parenting style, you will see ways to combine lessons and enrich teachable moments. As you focus on noticing the good, on being grateful, honest, and open, you will see benefits in your interactions with your children and in improved behaviors.

Learning new things takes time, practice and, yup, mistakes. Be forgiving of yourself as you work to tweak the way you do things in your family or as you introduce new ideas into your family culture. There will be triumphant days and aggravating days, joyful moments and disastrous moments. Small successes build upon one another - celebrate them. Learn from the parenting oops-es and keep moving forward.

Have patience. Patience with yourself, with your family and with your kids. Parenting is a process, an every day, every week, month, year, decade process of growth, frustrations, revelations, and joys. The Naked Parenting goal is that, by applying these ideas, you can feel more self-assured as a parent. Then, as you continue to put in the hard work, because of previous efforts, you're able to enjoy the process more and reap the rewards of well-adjusted, resilient and confident kids.

As you shift and adjust things within your family, remember this is a long-term timeline. Don't expect dramatic transformations all at once. However, I do believe that with implementation of different aspects of Naked Parenting, you can see immediate results in a variety of ways while you simultaneously teach, guide, and build on these principles for the future.

Naked Parenting really works. In an oddly timely way, just today, our oldest daughter came to me to share a story. Her observations impressed and humbled me. Her words are the best endorsement I could receive.

"Mom, at my age I'm starting to realize that people parent their kids very differently and some of it isn't too wonderful," she began almost dropping me out of my seat. She then explained that her friend was supposed to be grounded all weekend but had been allowed to do a list of fun things both Saturday and Sunday with friends. "You would never do that. If I were grounded, I would be grounded," she concluded rightly.

I asked, "How do you feel about that?"

"Well, I wouldn't like it," she admitted, "but I would change. If you tell me enough, eventually what I'm taught becomes habit and then I start to realize that other people don't have that happen. I can see the differences both positively and negatively and learn from that."

Whoa! That's encouragement for me to keep at it, to dive into the everyday knowing that as hard as it can be sometimes, the kids really are hearing and learning the lessons.

Your kids are worth it. You and your family are worth it. Good parenting takes effort, work and energy that we don't always feel we can muster, but your family is worth it. In our non-stop, busy, rushed lives, take the time to add Naked Parenting to your to-do list. Spend a little time each day to practice something you learned, or add a new tradition, reward system or set of expectations.

Here's a big high five to you - you're doing great! Go out and get Naked!

Action Request

Thank you for reading *Naked Parenting*. Please take a moment to review *Naked Parenting*, your feedback matters!

I would love to hear from you. What parts of *Naked Parenting* would you like to learn more about? How is *Naked Parenting* transforming your family?

Visit www.motherscircle.net to let me know.

Thank you!

BONUS MATERIAL

The most important thing that parents can teach their children is how to get along without them.

- Frank A. Clark

Family Rules

Follow these rules wherever you are, whoever you're with.

- No Complaining – be Grateful instead!

- Use Nice, Big-Kid Voices

- Be Trustworthy – always honest!

- Be Respectful – of each other, of our home

- Be Responsible – do lists & jobs on your own

- Be Fair – share, listen to each other's needs

- Be Caring – kind brothers & sisters & friends

- Be Courteous – good manners, be thoughtful, clean up after yourself

Character Counts! Make good choices.

Do the right thing even if no one is watching.

Try to do a little better today
than you did yesterday.

Everyone makes mistakes. If you make one, apologize, fix
it and go back to the rules.

Naked Parenting Goal Form

Name_____

Goal Month_____

Specific Goal_____

Will achieve by_____(date)

Daily and Weekly mini-goals to help you get there:

_____

_____

Daily: _____

_____

_____

Daily: _____

_____

_____

Weekly: _____

_____

_____

Weekly: _____

_____

_____

☐ I DID IT!

☐ I almost did it!

☐ I'm still working on it.

Date Achieved:_____

How did you feel working toward your goal? _____

_____

_____

How did you feel getting there? _____

_____

_____

What did you learn in working toward your goal? What
made you successful?_____

_____

_____

_____

_____

What, if anything, would you do differently? What could
you improve?_____

_____

_____

_____

What do you need to do to achieve your goal if you didn't
this month?_____

_____

_____

Paper Chains to Motivate and Reward Kids

A simple idea in college motivated a group of 17-21 year old women to earn top grades on campus, so I'm thinking this could really work for younger kids as a reward system or as extra inspiration in school work.

When I was the Scholarship Chair for my sorority in college, I cut up bunches of colorful strips of construction paper then I shared my plan. Anyone who got an A on a quiz, test or major paper could add their name to the A-Chain. Our goal was to have this paper chain grow along the stairway from the main floor to the third floor of our house by the end of the term. I couldn't have anticipated the positive response. Everyone excitedly jumped on board and proudly wrote their names and shared their successes with one another. We not only hit the top floor midway through the term, but we went all along the third floor hallway and headed down the back stairs! That year, our chapter was number one in grade point average; it was a rewarding achievement for us all.

It dawned on me that this could really work to motivate and reward kids, from toddler to teens. Here are a few ideas to use a paper chain in your family. To make paper chains, cut strips of construction paper then loop then through one another using glue, tape, or I prefer staples.

You could write the child's name on each strip along with a kind act they did or a chore they completed. Try color coding the strips by child and they can earn a strip whenever they listen the first time or put their shoes on by themselves. It could serve as a potty training tool and your toddler can pick out a link for going to the potty, perhaps a special patterned paper or one with stickers for poop. I can see this working with grades, practicing an instrument, cleaning bedrooms or just about anything a parent wants to focus on in their family.

Try to loop a chain around a kitchen counter, along a child's bedroom ceiling, or from one end of the house to another. Get creative and if your kids are older, get them involved in choosing their colors, attaching their link to the chain or in deciding what earns them a link. A little external motivation that costs nothing but a bit of time can really pay off in results.

As parents, it's always helpful to have new ideas for our tool bag, it seems that one reward system or motivational tool works for only so long, then it's time to change things up. This is a fun alternative to a good ol' sticker chart – and you could even use stickers on a link before adding it to the chain.

The paper chain reward is another way to help us look out for and see the good things our kids do. I need those reminders, especially when I fall into a pattern of harping on all the things they didn't do.

Nurturing the Couple

Taking time to communicate with your spouse or parenting partner and nurturing that relationship is vital in building and strengthening family relationships. A close family requires a close bond between people raising them, the heads of household.

Whatever form your family takes, whether is merged with step-children, half siblings or adoptive children, whether you have two mommies or a traditional mom and dad family, communication and connection between a family's parents is vital. If you're parenting singly, take time for yourself. For the purposes of our discussion, I refer to parenting teams as couples.

Studies show that couples spend less time together than they have in past decades, and spend only 10% of their time together. Within that small 10% of time, togetherness is often spent watching TV instead of really connecting.

Remember that long after the children are gone, you'll have each other, or that's the goal! To achieve that, you can't put your relationship on hold while you raise your children, it must be cared for consistently.

In my work, I see many couples struggle with this around the time of adding a baby to the family, or as life gets busy with teen children's schedules. Life shifts to become so kid-focused that too often the parents lose their bond in the shuffle.

The number-one technique to stay close is to communicate. Really make the time to talk openly, honestly, and in depth about, not just what's happening in your life, but what you're feeling. Talk about yourselves and your needs, not just about the baby or children.

Initiate discussions about a disappointment you may be feeling or about a hoped-for dream that you see slipping away. Brainstorm ways together that you can work toward your goal. If something is frustrating you in your family, don't push it down, expose it and air it out. I hear of so many misunderstandings, moms and dads who feel unheard; don't let those annoyances build and escalate, create a culture in your relationship in which emotions can be explored and shared in a nonjudgmental, safe environment.

Build-in time together, date nights can be going out somewhere or they can be close to home. Take a walk around the neighborhood, take a bath together with candles once the kids are in bed, do a favorite activity together over which you can talk. Puzzles, board games, or even working out together allows for time to talk. Just being together for focused time without other distractions is valuable and unifying.

One friend of mine told me that when her, now adult, kids were young, every Friday, she would feed and bathe the kids very early and have them in bed when her husband walked in the door. Friday night was for the two of them. It was a set weekly date, a time to nurture their relationship.

Sex matters. Couples who have regular intimacy are closer, feel happier and more satisfied in their relationships and are even physically healthier. It may seem unsavory or stodgy to schedule sex into your lives, but it can also work well. Flirt and send messages to one another throughout the day, the building anticipation is an added benefit. Make-out and snuggle up. When's the last time you really kissed each other, not just the unmemorable brush against the cheek on the way out the door, but real slow, romantic kissing?

Other ideas are to keep a notebook in your bedroom where you write notes back and forth to one another. Use it to share why you're grateful for your partner, write what makes him a great dad or what makes her an amazing mom, or perhaps send good wishes for a big presentation at work. Send cards or love notes to each other, either hidden in a desk, an underwear drawer or mailed to the house. A hand-written note is so meaningful and shows you took time. Another version of this continuing communication thread is to text throughout the day, or use an instant message application (Skype, Facebook, Google). I know of one couple who texts each other song lyrics using only emoticons. They try to stump each other and have a lot of laughs together, even when they're apart.

Laughing together builds closeness. Sharing private jokes, reminiscing about your past, sharing a funny story you heard on the radio, or even watching old family movies can get you cracking up together. Be playful!

Think back to when you were first together. You probably were polite with one another. Keeping manners up between a couple isn't formal, but instead it let's your spouse know that you're noticing their effort, that you're appreciative of whatever he/she just did. Sure, it may be dad's assigned job to take out the garbage or mow the lawn, but how would he feel if you just took a moment to say, "The lawn looks great! Thanks!" Maybe mom is home all day with the kids, an endless, thankless job, and it would be so powerful and connective to acknowledge that and express your gratitude for her.

Don't just assume that your partner knows it, say it. Tell them, thank them. Everyone thrives and feels good by being recognized for their actions so don't stop because you've been married for five years or together for twenty. Send a thank you note occasionally, leave a Post-It message in the pantry or in the garbage can underneath the bag where it can be discovered when the garbage is taken out.

Do something creative together: redecorate a room in the house, go to a paint-your-own pottery studio, write a children's book, compose a song. Do something physical together: go for a hike, take a dance class, take a morning walk or an evening bike ride, or enjoy a roll in the hay.

Support each another's projects and dreams, allow each partner time to themselves, eat by candle light, share your high and low points at bedtime each night, hold hands. Say, "I love you." Say it over and over, feel it and mean it. Treat each other as best friends; give without expectation of getting, listen and really hear. Share your heart and thoughts, protect the others' feelings, guide without judging, and check-in over coffee.

Trite expressions become so because they hold some truth. It's good advice to never go to bed angry, stay up and talk it through. It's true that love is in the details. Attention to details and what specifically matters to your partner, whether or not it matters to you, shows caring.

Make time together with your parenting partner a priority. Build regular one-on-one time into your schedules. As John Wooden says in *A Lifetime of Observations and Reflections On and Off the Court*: "The best thing a father can do for his children is to love their mother." And the reverse is true, too, of course. Caring for yourselves as a couple is the best gift you can give your children.

Why You Need Mommy Time

Mommy time is a way to fill ourselves up to be able to be better in all of our roles. As Moms, we spend much of our days focused on kids. Kids' meals, kid's behaviors, kids' activities, kid's homework, kid's bathing, brushing, towel-dumping, rule-not-following, stop-touching-him stuff.

You deserve some grown-up time. Guilt-free parenting is my mantra and giving yourself time should be a priority on your to do list. Go ahead and do something to fill yourself up.

When we feel fulfilled and like our own lives are valuable independent of being someone's Mommy, we open ourselves to personal growth and in turn to being better mothers, wives, friends, and people.

You've heard the expression: "If Mama ain't happy, ain't no one happy." It's so often true, as moms, that we set the tone of the family. We set the example. We create the culture over the long term and create the mood in the short-term.

How we greet the day and the people in our homes matters to the family culture. We are the key in sculpting the family dynamics and when we feel whole as women, we are better able to weather the tedium and build the home-lives we imagined when we first dreamed of a family.

So here's a quick list of some ideas for Mommy Time to

get you thinking about what you can do for yourself. Start today!

- Dig in your garden – for me, time in my garden is so peaceful and rejuvenating

- Get a manicure – or take the time to paint your own nails

- Take a bath – add a favorite fragrance

- Try out Tabata trainings

- Plan a special date night

- Pick up an old hobby you've been missing

- Take up a new hobby you've been interested in trying (knitting, painting, singing)

- Pack a picnic

- Arrange flowers and put them where you will see them often

- Go to a book club – yes, you can make time for reading as part of your Mommy Time!

- Play a mindless game of Candy Crush or Scramble on your phone (guilt-free)

- Get creative – paint, sculpt clay, write a poem

- Pour a cup of tea and just be

- Play an instrument

- Bake pretty cupcakes for dessert

- Learn a new language – you can listen to the lessons little by little

- Get a massage – even every so often can do wonders

- Write in a gratitude journal

- Meet a friend for a walk in the neighborhood, for breakfast out or an evening glass of wine

- Enjoy your favorite yoga class

- Watch a movie – who cares if it's the afternoon?

- If you like entertaining, plan a dinner party, the preparations can be a fun creative outlet

- Take a run

- Dance

- Read a magazine – save the parenting mags and read something that is all about your non-Mommy passions

- Meditate or pray

- Take a nap (I love a quick afternoon nap to perk me up for the rest of the day)

- Pause. Smile. Breathe.

Make time for Mommy Time! Do something that makes you feel like your authentic self, something that makes you smile and shine. You deserve it. Do it without guilt and without regret. Enjoy something just for you today. Give yourself the gift on your own time a little bit each day.

About the Author

Leah DeCesare's main gig is mother of three and she writes between car pools and laundry. Her pre-baby professional experience was in public relations and event planning. For the past thirteen years, her career has focused on birth, babies, and early parenting as a certified childbirth educator, a birth and postpartum doula.

Married for two decades, Leah's current parenting adventures revolve around kids, elementary-aged through teenagers, creating the basis for her Mother's Circle parenting blog, www.motherscircle.net, where she shares perspectives on parenting from pregnancy through teens.

Working on her debut novel, Leah has also written articles for publication in the International Doula, The Key, and local publications and online outlets.

Leah spearheaded the Campaign for Hope to build the Kampala Children's Centre for Hope and Wellness in Uganda. Please visit www.kampalahope.org to learn more.

She parents, writes, teaches and volunteers in Rhode Island where she co-founded the nonprofit organization Doulas of Rhode Island in 2008.